T0042300

Tess Went to Work

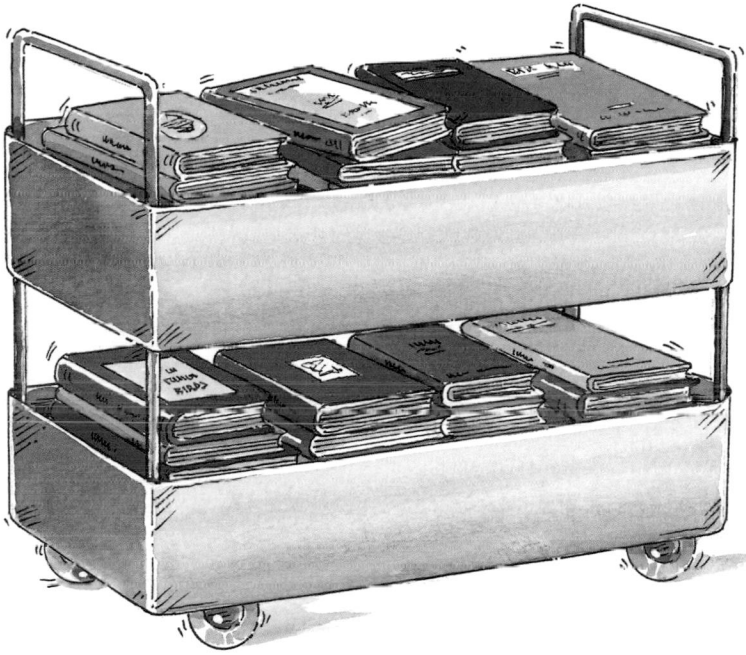

Martin Reed
Illustrated by Virginia Gray

One day, Tess went to work with her dad.

Library Hours
10:00 – 8:00 Monday to Friday
10:00 – 5:00 Saturday and Sunday

Dad helped people find books.

So did Tess.

Dad helped people use computers.

So did Tess.

Dad helped people check out books.

So did Tess.

Dad helped people put books away.

So did Tess.

"I had fun at work today," said Tess.

"So did I!" said Dad.